SUNRISES

A POETIC COLLECTION

by

Patricia Hochstetler

PATH BOOKS
Goshen, Indiana

Printed in the United States of America,
by Color House Graphics Inc.
Cover Photo by Patricia Hochstetler
Back Cover Photo by Mike Albin
Designed and Edited by Baker Trittin Press for Path Books

To order additional copies please
visit www.amishjewishcult.com
or write: Patricia's Books
            P.O. Box 1071
            Goshen, IN 46527
or E-mail path@maplenet.net
Call 574-202-7596 to leave contact information

Publishers Cataloging-Publication Data
Hochstetler, Patricia 1948-
        Sunrises
        Patricia Hochstetler - Goshen, Indiana
        Path Books, 2007

                p.   cm.

ISBN: 978-1-60530-587-5

Second Printing

DEDICATION

To my Lord and Savior who
enabled me to survive.

AUTHOR'S NOTE

Many of these poems are my first efforts in writing poetry beginning in 1995. It includes a mixture of some I have written in the last ten years while I was writing my life story of growing up in an Amish-Jewish cult.

Writing poetry helped ease tension while writing my autobiography.

Often a poem played out in my head and my hand somehow found a paper and pen. Soon another simple poem joined my collection.

May you find God's grace, mercy, and deliverance as you read these poems. Enjoy!

CONTENTS

9   Nature's Glow

10   Enlightening

11   Writer's Workshop Beauty

12   A Child Watching

13   Colors for You

14   My Pen

15   Forsaken

16   The Stem

17   My Rock

18   Lost and Found

20   Life for Life

22   A New Rainbow

24   Life Is a Work of Art

25   Time

26   Traffic of Life

28   Word Power

29   The Valley

30   Lord, I'm Yours

31   A Faceless Child

32   Rain Down Your Love

33   Orphan

34   Sunrises

35   The Middle

36   Love

37   Letters

38	Rejoice!
39	Multi-Dimensional
40	The Heartbeat
41	A Rainbow
42	The Star
43	Swanegan Creek
44	Aw Ba Sa (ABC) Done in Dutch and English
46	The Wheel of Life
47	Flying Dreams
48	Young Hope
49	Helping Others
50	Delivered
51	That's Life
52	Relief
53	Nature's Path
54	A Cone
55	A Secret
56	Why The Ten Commandments?
57	The Ten Commandments
58	Don't Feel Sorry!
59	A Journey
60	Feelings
61	Spring
62	Perfect Love and Deliverance

NATURE'S GLOW

The Window
open to sunlight
dashing in.
Its beauty
allowing
warmth,
peace
and love
to glow.

This is the first poem I ever wrote

ENLIGHTENING

The window of eyes open
letting in the beauty of
light and warmth.
Peace and love flow
enlightening
the soul.

This poem won the Editor's Choice Award with
The International Library of Poetry in September 2007.

My second poem

WRITER'S WORKSHOP BEAUTY

Writers Workshop
No beauty sleep
New faces and food
More knowledge

No beauty sleep
Less is more
More knowledge
Better feelings

Less is more
Beauty revealed
Better feelings
Better writing

Beauty revealed
New faces and food
Better writing
Writers Workshop

My third poem

A CHILD WATCHING

As a child I walked
with silent bare feet among
many rough hills, jagged valleys
and raging waters.

Green forest walls
surrounding shy earth,
shock tunneling from golden meadows
to blue sky that felt healing.

Sitting quietly on rocks looking up
waiting, listening, and watching,
I found God's blessings in simple trees, birds and clouds
while adoring His peaceful creations.

Colors for You

Lord paint your students
with your colors

Give them hearts of gold
bless them with rainbow minds

Make their voices pure hues of you
and tongues glistening in song to spread your word

Provide them with beautiful springs of joy for you
and clear feelings for others

Arm your people with a visible spirit of service
and color attitudes as snow

Splatter their hands sparkling to serve you
and speed fluorescent feet to light your path and run for you

Quilt them together with your colorfast handiwork of love
gild them with the bright tints of your Son

Help all students to serve you
with your most colorful reflections

MY PEN

My pen faithful day and night,
when called upon you bounce
memories on command.

Jotting down words that sing
and dance on paper
all day.

Jotting down words that sing
and dance on paper
all night.

Jotting down words that sing
and dance on paper
How does it feel?

Are you speaker, writer or hero?
Does your back ache?
Is your spine squeezed too hard or tight?

Have you written too many long hours?
You never complain.
You tell the story for waiting ears.

You reveal what happens, satisfying curious minds.
You give delight to people near and far.
Dependable you spread God's word and glory on paper.

Thank you my friend, my pen.

FORSAKEN

She is lonely.
Will company come?

She is quiet.
Will she respond?

She is hungry
Will she eat?

She is patient.
Will she give up?

She is lame.
Will she heal?

She waits!
How long can she linger?

Why is she injured?
She suffered broken bones and spirit.

THE STEM

At ground level looking up the arched stem,
The power of life so strong yet fragile.
Reaching through the air serial unfolds with time.
The stem carries life as an umbilical cord to the future.

Lively green leaves of shade wave life and protection.
Stems lead to glimmers of hope and hues of life.
A backbone to future growth
Can we climb? Can we climb to the top?

Thorns as daggers and spears wait to jab us,
We choose to avoid their points and dangers.
Using their foundations like ladder rungs to climb
Pressing on to a steadfast advance
moving forward to the roses.

The stem a bridge will be to beauty above,
life, buds and roses.
Soft petals of hope yet solid stepping stones to the future.
Life develops new roots, taller growth, and larger blossoms.
Carried by grace we choose to prevail.

MY ROCK

Jesus is the solid rock in my life.
I marvel at the strength of my rock.
Like a rock, Jesus is my strong foundation.

On my rock, I stand secure.
On my rock, I sit in peace.
I kneel knowing Jesus loves me.

Jesus is the rock of my faith,
He saved me and helps me grow.
My rock is the stepping stone to my future.

This I know.

Lost and Found

Lost
    that child wanders
      a muse of stars
        a moon that sees
          water?
            what to eat?
            sticks and stones
            all alone

                How far?
                 fear that believes...
                   desperation the truth
                   hope the highest
                   what's priority?
                   lost for real
                     the fact exists
                       total surrender

                Found
                feelings of relief
              the sun shines
                clouds disappear in blue sky
            drinks plentiful
         food galore
       appetite restores
      You do! You don't! What to do?

This is
    My story
        Jesus found me first
        I obtained faith
            received Him
                true love I experienced
                grace, mercy
                    and salvation.

Now I stand firmly centered on my rock foundation

LIFE FOR LIFE

A blue heron dropped from the trees one sunny spring day,
Landing softly at the edge of the pond.
He slowly waded in staring at the water,
Then disappeared under the water surface for a moment.

He popped up, a bright orange ribbon dangled in his mouth,
So we thought.
Will the heron build a nest with that colorful ribbon?
His slow steps returned him to the grass.

With a couple snaps of the beak on the ground,
The ribbon curled and fanned on one end,
Then flopped like a fish out of water.
We realized the orange ribbon was a gold fish.

In a few gulps the fish disappeared.
A couple swallows, then a drink!
The heron stood straight, quiet and satisfied.
We watched in awe.

How long would the fish live inside the heron?
I thought of Jonah swallowed and inside a big fish,
After witnessing this golden fish swallowed by the large bird.
I thought of Jesus, our precious Savior,
hung on the old rugged cross.

Jesus, the Son of God, beat by man and nailed up to die.
How long did Jesus hang in despair before death?
Why did God allow Jonah to return from darkness and live?
Sometimes we ask why we suffer!

All in God's plan, He allowed a life taken for life given.
His people, His Son, His fish, His heron, all His creations!
The fish died for the heron to live,
Christ died for us to live eternally.
What is our lot in life?

Do we give anything for others to live,
Or continually take for ourselves?
Does living in spiritual darkness cause spiritual death?
What is our part in life and death?

Are we prepared for whatever God allows
to happen in our life?

A NEW RAINBOW

God made a new rainbow
I no longer see dark clouds
New colors brighten my life
Hues sent by God with hope
God promises not to destroy
But to save eternally

I see a new rainbow
I see a new rainbow
I see a new rainbow

I no longer see darkness
No more deluge
Rather floods of living water
To quench thirst of the soul
Love with a sound of suffering
Jesus gave himself for you and me

I see a new rainbow
I see a new rainbow
I see a new rainbow

God sent His Son for you and me.
Love lights my life each day.
A promise beyond imagination!
A crown of thorns He wore,
Life gone, a mothers tears.
Jesus rose from the dead.

I see a new rainbow
I see a new rainbow
I see a new rainbow

Love makes my life beam daily
Jesus put a song in my heart
A song of praise and forgiveness
A song of freedom and blessing
A song of redemption and salvation
I no longer see darkness

I see a new rainbow
I see a new rainbow
I see a new rainbow

God promises not to destroy by water
This is love, that others may live
Jesus died for you and me giving us grace
Free saving grace if we believe and accept Him
A rainbow promise of eternal life to faces of every color
The new rainbow of God's colors in His kingdom

A new rainbow I see
A new rainbow I see
A new rainbow I see

LIFE IS A WORK OF ART

Life is a work of art.
It's up to me how
I paint my picture.
Will it look stark or smart?

The tapestry I brush,
With strokes of love and manner,
Life begins as a work of art.
Shaping all scenes, don't rush!

I spread colors across,
Each path connects every point.
Life is a work of art,
Painted by the painting boss.

Think ahead of the brush and follow the laws.
How will I deal with mistakes?
Life is a continuous work of art.
Are there many or few flaws?

Will I want another start?
Is there a need to erase?
Life is a work of art.
One chance to create the best part.

Will faith make my picture glow?
What will my decisions show?
Life is a work of art to the end,.
Will my history of life art have a beautiful flow?

TIME

Time walks by
no replacement
a deaf sound.

Silent dust
settles on your heart
to stay

No key
no questions
no answers
that will
turn back
the time.

Time and life
march on.

TRAFFIC OF LIFE

People often drive as they feel. Feeling frustrated how do you drive? Do you act as if you have a fly rod in hand and want to catch every moving vehicle and throw them behind you and go for the next reel? Are you driving your life or is life driving you?

How do you drive when you're in love, happy, sad, scared, disappointed, depressed, worried, hurt, anxious or impatient? Does road rage consume you? Do you act like a raging ocean and swallow all on the surface? Are you happy singing tunes as you flow along? Does your driving mirror you?

These feelings produce actions—some safe, some unsafe. Watch vehicles on the road and see results of drivers' feelings and personalities without seeing the drivers. Some zoom by, but later in reflections of red, they sit in front of a police car or lay rolled in a ditch. Others you see miles down the road or in the next state steadily cruising along. Which category do you fit?

Feelings often get people in trouble on highways and on the road of life. They miss the best roads, exits, signs and other people. Our feelings and actions result in memories, rewards of safety, or crashes, scares, and careless games with high costs, all is history. Signals and warnings are apparent. We can learn from others the costs of actions. How is your traffic of life?

Inner peace, good self-esteem, confidence and alertness make the difference on freeways or the road of life. At home do we act as bulls butting down all in our way when we feel bad, or can we control ourselves in an orderly fashion? Does your life flow as you feel?

How would it be if Christ were in the driver's seat? On the highway or on the path of life, what would he do? Where would he go or take us and how would he drive? Could you follow his footsteps? If we accept him, he wants us to do our best to follow him. He did the rest and will forgive us with all grace and understanding if we ask Him.

Life is like traffic, ever changing. People flow in and out of our lives, some bump into us, others pass us or lag behind, others flow with us, while some jerk us around playing their mind games. Can we stay on a steady pace to our final destination and praise God for the traffic lessons in life? Enjoy your journey!

Word Power

With written words I feel powerful,
yet weak with grammar, punctuation and spoken words.
I can make a story dance on the page.

Description jingles and jangles to the beat of many words.
Colors reflect on all sides, each line and every scene.
Words bounce from brain to paper
quickly whispering the untold.

Words flow gracefully as a deer waltzing along,
clearing a fence and continuing for the next bite.
It's easy as one, two, three!

I love the power of words, the more the merrier,
until the story unfolds and is completely told.
Let others edit, prune, cut, rearrange, and toss around.

Words open doors and blinds,
take off the shades and turn on the lights.
Words reveal true experiences to help others grow.

I will march on to another tune,
the next scene and more words.
My rock foundation, God, is my strength
even in every word.

THE VALLEY

I'm walking through the valley.
Lord, be with me in this dark vale.

Carry me through despair.
Be my footprints!

Lift me high over low terrain.
Shadow me with mercy and grace.

Put me on eagles wings,
help me soar.

Bless me with mountains someday,
shower me with your love and strength.

I will always praise and glorify you.

LORD, I'M YOURS

Lord, I'm Yours, use my eyes to see You
in your intricately created handiwork.
Give me sight to discern what's right. Help me light the days
So the world can see You and praise Your Holy name.

God, I'm Yours, use my ears
to hear Your choice words.
Give me wisdom to know Your will. Help me guide others
To the cross and show the world Your sac - ri - fice.

Christ, I'm Yours, use my nose
to smell your life flowers.
Give me blossoms to show Your love. Make me fertile soil
In fragrant fields of harvest with Your springs of new life.

Savior, I'm Yours, use my tongue
to taste and spread Your marvelous works.
Give me a voice of praise for You. Help me tell of
You're marvelous works and Your free gift of sal - va - tion.

Master, I'm Yours, use my hands
to touch Your loving people.
Give me love to show Your glory. Em - power me with
Your joyful blessings, mold me, make me more like You and
use me.

A Faceless Child

My God's hand protected me,
A faceless child.
Life hard, as a child slave,
Work only, punishments not mild.

My Lord's mercy touched me,
An emotionless child.
My woes and mistakes,
You saw and forgave and never filed a reference.

You were my guide through life.
A blind child, I felt my way holding your hand.
You led me through rough waters,
the hard times and mild ones.

You gave me a hidden courage.
An ego-stripped child, you stood tall by my side,
I looked up.
When I remained sober, you smiled.

You blessed me and gave me a face,
emotions, sight, ego, deliverance and a home.
A rejected orphan child,
You adopted me giving me a face and I smiled.

You are my father, guide and redeemer.
A deafened child, someday you will give me a voice.
Thank you for sparing my life,
and giving me the face of a child.

RAIN DOWN YOUR LOVE

Rain down your love on me.
Oh Lord, help me grow in you.
Melt away my fears,
Fill me with your hope.

Rain down your love on me.
Settle the storms in my heart,
give me peace.
Help me see your mercy and grace.

Rain down your love,
hold my hand as we walk together.
Shower me with words of wisdom,
and open my mouth to praise you.

Rain down your love and give me a new life.
Bring me kindness and joy.
Quench my thirst with your water of life.
Help me feel your love on earth.

Rain down your love on me.
Mold me into your vessel.
A vessel of water to refresh others.
A cistern to last for you.

ORPHAN

An orphan in my own home,
parents present in body, gone in mind.

What can I do without being punished?
What must I do to prevent trouble?

A weed I'll remain waiting to be chopped down.
Like grass I grow learning to wait on the Lord.

Placed in a foreign world and orphan I stayed,
until the Lord adopted me and welcomed me into His family.

Now a loving father I have.
How wonderful it is to trust God more than man.

Happy Father's Day,
to my father, Lord and Savior.

An orphan no more,
I've been adopted.

SUNRISES

The sense of beginning
The start of a day
The first of sun or insight

Anticipation of a brighter future
Hope for a new day
Another chance to see more in life

A peek at a majestic scene
Ever changing moments
Sunrises reveal the secrets of the night

When one begins to see the light
Your day lights up
Colors develop and change

First watch the horizon of hope
The sky lightens
Formations appear

Sometimes clouds roll by
Quiet stillness of the dark turns to light
Action! Things happen

Life is much like sunrises

THE MIDDLE

In life I've stood in the middle.
I also stood in the middle of a rainbow.

In both places I looked all around for brilliant colors.
I stood in the middle of the rainbow.

The sun shined brightly.
Raindrops fell lightly.

Brightness glowed in silver tones,
and there I stood in the middle of the rainbow.

I knew I stood in the middle of a rainbow,
too close to see all the colors.

I ran outside the raindrops
and saw all the rainbow colors.

I ran back in the middle of the rainbow
and saw only silver raindrops glowing.

The magical glory of God shone
inside the middle of the rainbow as well as outside.

In the middle of the rainbow I stood
and felt complete peace and saw beauty in a different way.

I am the middle child.

LOVE

The most excellent way is love.
If people speak of God and
have no love they are
as a gong or clanging cymbal.

If they have knowledge and prophecy
and faith to move mountains
but have not love,
there's no gain.

Love is patient and kind, without envy and strife,
not boasting, proud, rude or self-seeking.
Love is not easily made angry
and keeps no records of wrong.

Love will not delight in evil but rejoices in truth.
Love protects, gives hopes and perseveres.
Humans see poor reflections in a mirror.
True love never fails as Christ proved.

His love is the greatest.

LETTERS

We are letters, and letters can kill or bring life.
We write on hearts and are read by everybody.
We show what we are.

The results of Christ,
written by the Holy Spirit not only on stone,
but on human hearts for others to read.

This confidence is ours
through Christ, not of ourselves.
It comes from God who gives life.

What kind of letters
Are we writing for others?
Think about it!

REJOICE!

Rejoice in the Lord, always rejoice!
Let gentleness be evident.
God is near.
Rejoice!

Be not anxious in anything,
but in everything, with prayer
and petition and with thanksgiving
present your requests to God.

The peace of God, which transcends all understanding
will guide your heart
and your mind in Christ.
Rejoice!

Christ's perfection made
imperfections disappear
through forgiveness.
Rejoice!

MULTI-DIMENSIONAL

Life is multi-dimensional.
How long is God's choice.
How high and wide is your choice.

Faith adds length.
Hope brings new heights.
Love broadens everybody in all ways.

Remember—add a cup of discernment!
My friend, if life is still black and white,
and without beauty, add a big bottle of joy for color.

Then life will surely be multi-dimensional.

THE HEARTBEAT

As a stone,
I stand alone.

God remains the rock.
The Rock under my feet.

I hear God's heartbeat
and listen to His Word in the heat.

I know God lives in my heart.
Now I can serve as His hands, feet and voice.

God's heartbeat echoing in my ears
throbs with my own.

I'm not alone.

A Rainbow

If you want a rainbow,
you must color your
world with beauty.

The beauty of joy,
laughter and friendliness
will brighten the world for all.

A balance of peace and
understanding will give you
rainbow colored memories.

Life rainbows are made by
a choice to bring positive
beauty into your life.

THE STAR

Jesus is the star of my life.
He is my hero and Savior.

He gives me light
by day and night.

He directs me on
the path of life.

SWANEGAN CREEK

The waters of Swanegan creek,
Cold refreshing springs rushing
To nowhere it seemed.

Shallow wading for hot dirty feet,
Even a cool bath could make one feel
squeaky clean and ready for a warm bed.

Satisfying thirsty people and gardens,
water for cooking and keeping food cool,
this beautiful creek served many well.

Yet, the calmness and quietness of
Swanegan creek could not put peace
in the hearts and minds of mankind.

Children could feel the joys of this creek
and see the beauty it brought into life
as it threaded through the village land.

Please Swanegan creek, flow peace
and freedom into our region.
Bring joy and blessings, take away fear and strife.

Even the great quiet gorgeous Swanegan creek
had no power or influence to alter
man's thinking; only one little girl's.

A Pennsylvania - Dutch poem

BISHT DO GRONK?

Aw Ba Sa
Do maust sue de gama ga

Flyickt bish do gronk.
Von do vit nat fa ga,

Sell maint as do con nat essa.
Do con nat middauck essa.

Meah han hingel on nep
Mit greena bona fa fresa.

Bish do fa de gama ga
vo de liet switza ofa Yasu?

Ich huff as do gain
Soo do dut nat baul va speida.

Denocht, meah huffa fa
rech free soo haim fa de gama.

ARE YOU SICK?

ABC
You must go to church.

Maybe you are sick.
If you don't want to go.

That means you can't eat.
You can't eat dinner.

We'll have chicken and dumplings
with green beans to feast on.

Are you going to church
Where the people talk of Jesus?

I hope you go
So you won't feel stomach pain.

Tonight, we hope to be home
from church early.

THE WHEEL OF LIFE

Round and round turns the wheel of life.
The mind tells the feet to track, a circle head to toe.
The eyes see a need, the hands help,
a circle face to fingers.

The ears hear words and sounds, the mouth speaks,
a circle from two ears to a mouth
and on to many more ears,
multiplying God's Word of salvation.

A living testimony of faith, hope and love,
where one life touches many others, a full circle from
God to Christ and mankind,
and from generation to generation.

Round and round goes the wheel of life,
with Christ at the helm.
From God through Christ came love, mercy and grace.
It's up to us to choose Him for a full circle of eternal life with
God.

FLYING DREAMS

A dream so real,
Always able to fly above trees.
This leaves great appeal.

Often a small jump, up, up and away,
Drifting free, drifting me,
A feeling never forgotten.

Weekly flying dreams caused
me to wonder,
can I really fly?

With baling twine, I tied up fabric and tarps,
stiffened by twigs tightly fastened to my arms,
now wings I have to fly.

Like a bird see me fly,
circle around, look down,
flying free I'll be.

Jump off a big log, flap, flap, flap, nothing worked.
My body seemed made of lead.
Waiting for a puff of wind I try again. Nothing!

So I waited for that next flying dream,
In those free butterfly dreams, oh what joy I felt for years.

YOUNG HOPE

Young and innocent,
You know things must change.

Hope keeps you going,
You pray for a better tomorrow.

Belief that good is coming someday,
Makes the day bearable.

Waiting on the Lord, the only answer you know,
You hear and see wrong prevail.

How long can this continue?
You must wait silently in pain.

Your mute tongue shouts inside.
When will it end?

Patience and fear keeps you prisoner.

HELPING OTHERS

There's no better feeling than helping another.
Offering two hands to meet a need
gives great joy to receiver and giver.

A listening ear brings peace to the misunderstood.
Taking time to provide needs
for others helps all feel good.

Volunteer to experience the thrill.
You can be a blessing as well as
give others blessings of goodwill.

DELIVERED

Hearing the thunder and seeing the storm, I struggled.
Unable to swim, You served as my buoy.

Lord, you heard my cry and delivered me
from drowning in the swirl.

I will forever thank and glorify You,
my father and Savior.

I'm triple delivered, birth,
a second chance in life, and through salvation.

THAT'S LIFE

At the end of the storm,
A rainbow forms.

Feel the storm beat.
Then know the peace.

See the rainbow colors,
Time viewing is rewarding.

Rise and shine!
Your face sunny and bright!

The storm is past,
Don't look back

Seize the moments!
See the beauty all around.

That's life,
Full of storms, peace and beauty.

It's a choice what to do,
how to feel, and what to see.

What's your choice?

RELIEF

Our smallest house meant relief.
Rush in and hold our breath,
Stench bad enough to gag a maggot.

Hoping wasps perched on nests near the hot tin roof won't
Dive for our face or any other bare skin
As we sit on a hole waiting for relief.

A Sears catalog lay near to aid, after relief came.
No windows, few cracks or vents,
And many cobwebs hung.

Can you imagine sitting in this little house?
The urge to exit
As strong as the one to enter.

Buzzing blow flies circle.
Bare skin exposed to the elements,
Hot or cold, one waited for relief.

Once relief came, we dashed out the door
Of the outhouse for a breath of air,
As thankful to leave as to enter.

NATURE'S PATH

Nature's path applies no golden rules
and promises no flowers.

Never asking forgiveness,
nature is not understandable.

Leaving a path
for researchers to follow.

Experts baffled in the array
of rudeness left.

Having no respect the sting
and drama unfolds.

People are hostage to mother nature,
who rudely alters lives and routes.

Snuffing out life in the twinkle of an eye.
The twist of death lies at hand.

Destruction! Look all directions
and see life and death mixed.

The situation in God's hands
the green and gold fall valueless.

Hail vanishes and
Rain like teardrops flow.

Helpless people cut to the heart
as the wrath of nature prevails.

53

A CONE

A sweet cone,
Like a pear turned upside down
Smooth, cold, flavorful ice cream
Placed neatly into a crunchy
Cylinder shaped brown waffle cone.

Tasty in the mouth,
Satisfying in the belly
Giving the tongue good exercise.
Oh, the pleasure of a cone.

A SECRET

When I first started writing,
I felt driven to tell a secret untold story.
Like a dream when sound asleep,
Can I unleash my muted tongue,
After so many years?

My pen and fingers served as speakers.
God stepped in as director.
I watched and listened as words for others to read
Unraveled from the tapestry of
My memory and threaded onto paper.

The story rang loud in my ears of
A little girl I once knew long ago.
Her hidden story of escape and life restoration
Must be shared to help humans
Have a more fulfilled life.

The story does not belong to me.
I'm only a tool used in the process of delivery.
The message is to honor and glorify
Our maker, Jesus Christ, who wants
The best for all His people.

WHY THE TEN COMMANDMENTS?

Imagine what our world
would be like if no one
kept the Ten Commandments?

People killing at will.
Everything available stolen!
Adultery committed in every home.

Freedom to covet everything!
People serving anything as their God.
Anyone could be a false witness against you.

Many graven images made and worshiped as God.
God's name used in vain anywhere anytime.
Never a day to rest!

No guides for human behavior!
Existing mankind animal-like constantly.
No honoring parents!

Is this a world you would want to live in?
No faith or faithful!
Where would you find peace and comfort?

Why the Ten Commandments?

THE TEN COMMANDMENTS

God gave the Ten Commandments
to Moses as a guide for his people.
Imagine the peace and
comfort felt if everybody were moral?

No killing, theft, adultery or coveting,
Serving no other Gods or graven images. No false witnesses!
Parents always honored and a weekly day of rest enjoyed,
No taking God's name in vain.

God ordered Moses to write these commandments for
mankind to keep.
Faithfully following these commandments is rewarding.
The Ten commandments can be used to uphold or condemn.
By actions we can choose our own results.

God gave us rules because He loves us and for our good.
He wanted peace for us and those around us.
Would you like this kind of world?
Can you imagine the peace and comfort?

Do you want to keep the Ten commandments?
Do you want others to keep the Ten Commandments?

DON'T FEEL SORRY!

"I feel sorry for you," she said.
"Don't feel sorry for me!" I replied.
"My life made me who I am today and I'm thankful.
Thankful to be alive and enjoying life on earth."

Please think of me and treat me like other people.
God allowed my life to happen.
I never planned my parents, my name,
Relatives, where I lived, my school,
Or any of my childhood. That's past!

God must have a purpose for my life or
He would never have helped me survive.
So please don't feel sorry for me.
Just treat me like other people.
I live life looking forward not backwards.

Now, I have a choice,
I'm responsible for my decisions,
Actions, and thoughts.
I'm making up for lost time and
Living life to the fullest each moment and day.

Don't feel sorry for me!

A JOURNEY

How exciting to be on a journey!
No matter where we start it's always a learning experience.

Life is good, learning its mysteries one day at a time.
Not knowing what tomorrow will bring,
We can waste less time stewing and more planning.

Do we meet curves and crashes
Or turn and follow to the end?
Life is a challenge.

Can we meet a life bump and get over it?
When we trust God to get us over, around and through things
He leads us.
He knows our finish line and will help us reach it if we trust
Him.

When we anticipate and look for the next challenge,
We can say, "What's in it for me to learn?
What will the deliverance story be to tell?"

In each challenge there's a story
Everyone's life is a story.
They are all different and without set patterns.

God makes all our journeys interesting.

FEELINGS

Feeling trapped, alone,
No help in sight.

More obstacles arrive with time.
They took from me and there's no caring.

All caged am I.
No picnic!

Storms rise,
No light shining.

Silent, eyes blurry,
Hopeless, alone am I.

Pen in hand, words unravel
From the head and heart.

Expressions of feelings
Unfold the untold.

SPRING

New life begins all around.
Fresh tree leaves bud,
Trumpetlike daffodils bloom.

Baby animals appear.
Birds sing and chicks hatch.
Bees buzz for honey.

Blue sky brightens the earth.
Lovely clouds roll in and rain soaks the soil
Freshening green grass and plants to supply food.

Children run and play with delight.
Warmth returns and outside work begins.
Gardens flourish and grow.

Praise God for spring blessings.

PERFECT LOVE AND DELIVERANCE

God has no welfare system.
He has a fair plan system approach.
Love, mercy, grace and peace.

With love, God through His Son Jesus Christ,
Set guidelines for us by His examples and
Earthly path recorded in His Word — The Bible.

Believing Jesus Christ is born of God,
we accept God and His love.
Love for God is to obey His command.
This is victory that overcomes all, our faith in God and Christ.

As a caged orphan-like child of simple faith in God,
My heavenly Father chose me for an example of His perfect
love and deliverance.
Christ didn't return and labor and sacrifice for nothing.

I am living proof of His love.
God loves His children enough to make a way
against all odds.
As He did for me, He will do for you, if you believe in Him as
in I John 5:1-12.

God's welfare system is fair and free for asking.
He shows love, mercy and grace.
He gives peace.

Amen.